The
Caring Congregation
Ministry

Care Minister's Manual

Karen Lampe
Melissa Gepford

THE CARING
CONGREGATION
MINISTRY

Care Minister's Manual

Abingdon Press™
Nashville

THE CARING CONGREGATION MINISTRY:
CARE MINISTER'S MANUAL

Copyright © 2021 by Abingdon Press

ISBN 978-1-7910-1340-0

21 22 23 24 25 26 27 28 29 30 —10 9 8 7 6 5 4 3 2 1
MANUFACTURED IN THE UNITED STATES OF AMERICA

Contents

Introduction

The Caring Congregation Ministry is a model for person-to-person care that has been proven to work in small and large churches across the US. It is a laity-centered ministry, where laypersons receive rigorous training and then are commissioned to serve as Congregational Care Ministers, caring for others in their own congregation and their extended community.

The Implementation Guide is the main book for getting started. It introduces the ministry model and explains the Five Essentials that form the ministry's foundation. It is practical, full of checklists and other tools to help pastors and other leaders understand (and explain) this way of providing congregational care.

This is its companion book, the *Care Minister's Manual*, and is the personal training workbook and reference guide for Congregational Care Ministers (CCMs), who serve a central role in the Caring Congregation Ministry. CCMs receive in-depth training, where they learn the theological foundations of congregational care, plus the behaviors, habits, and practices they will need to follow in order to serve others well. Each CCM-in-training should have a copy of this manual. It serves as their training workbook, which then becomes the CCM's personal reference guide.

PART ONE

The Four Key Concepts and the Five Essentials

The Four Key Concepts and the Five Essentials

We were glad to share not only God's good news with you but also our very lives because we cared for you so much.

—1 Thessalonians 2:8

The Four Key Concepts

As you work your way through this book in order to establish your Congregational Care Ministry, you will encounter four key concepts that we emphasize throughout:

1. **Embrace teamwork.** There are no lone rangers in this ministry. Jesus had a team, and we need teams to help us be the community of faith we are called to be. *Build a team.*

2. **Trust the Holy Spirit.** You are never alone, and God will give you the tools you need for each situation; the Spirit will be leading you in every aspect of your ministry.

3. **Evaluate, evaluate, evaluate.** Do not be afraid of change; be afraid of not changing. Always be looking for new ways to keep your ministry effective and nimble.

4. In all things, pray first! Everything we do must be undergirded with prayerful discernment.

The Four Key Concepts

EMBRACE TEAMWORK

TRUST THE HOLY SPIRIT

EVALUATE

PRAY FIRST

The Five Essentials

One of my mentors and teachers said to me, "Karen, you can have people read the books and teach them through a seminar, but they need to understand the basics of organizing the ministry." This statement is so very true. As I have taught churches of all sizes across the country, it has become ever clearer to me that there are five essential steps for organizing this ministry. Each step is addressed in detail in the *Implementation Guide* and here in this *Manual*. As we begin, take a moment to consider how these steps might be addressed in your church:

Five Essentials For Organizing Your Care Ministry

1. **Recruit and Equip:** Choose and train the laity to become Congregational Care Ministers. Do not be afraid of empowering talented laity to use their gifts and graces. Training and deployment will take time, but it will be worth it! The church and community will be blessed beyond measure, and those who are trained will also find new purpose.

2. **Define Roles and Responsibilities:** Choose key volunteers who will help the pastor organize, triage, and deploy the other volunteers.

3. **Establish the Documentation System:** Create confidential documentation systems that may be in both electronic and paper formats.

4. **Evaluate:** Evaluate the current care needs of your church and community. Do you have support ministries that are effective? For instance, for the past many years, there has been an epidemic of new addictions across the country. Who are the champions who could help you develop a recovery ministry? Dream big about how you will offer care not only for individuals but also for all the people in your community.

5. **Build the Congregational Need:** You must establish your vision of care so that your congregation recognizes the need for this ministry and understands how it will succeed. Communicate to your congregation your excitement about the Congregational Care Ministers (CCMs) and the importance of the healing ministries of the church.

The Five Essentials

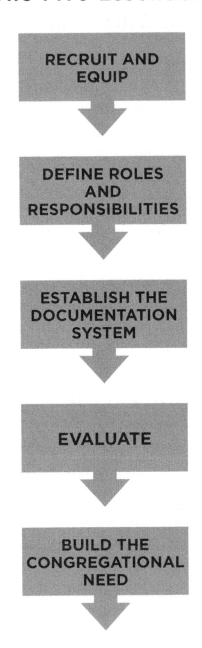

RECRUIT AND EQUIP

DEFINE ROLES AND RESPONSIBILITIES

ESTABLISH THE DOCUMENTATION SYSTEM

EVALUATE

BUILD THE CONGREGATIONAL NEED

Questions for Reflection

Before you begin the Congregational Care Minister training, take some time to consider and reflect, to prepare yourself for the task you are about to undertake. As you begin this ministry, consider the following questions:

- What is God calling you to do?

- How might your life experiences and story inform that calling?

- What are the resources that you need to initiate this ministry?

- Who can help you get organized?

Topics Covered throughout the Training

Theology of Care

In All Things, Pray First

Boundaries

Pastoral Listening and Spiritual Guidance

Visitation: The Most Sacred Hours

Leading Through the Darkest Valley

Organization

Caring for People in Crisis and Trauma

Mental Health Ministry

Recovery Ministry

Communal Trauma

Recruit and Equip

Christ is just like the human body—a body is a unit and has many parts; and all the parts of the body are one body, even though there are many. We were all baptized by one Spirit into one body, whether Jew or Greek, or slave or free, and we all were given one Spirit to drink. Certainly the body isn't one part but many. If the foot says, "I'm not part of the body because I'm not a hand," does that mean it's not part of the body? If the ear says, "I'm not part of the body because I'm not an eye," does that mean it's not part of the body? If the whole body were an eye, what would happen to the hearing? And if the whole body were an ear, what would happen to the sense of smell? But as it is, God has placed each one of the parts in the body just like he wanted.

—1 Corinthians 12:12-18

Pastors, it's time to get out of the way. The laity have been gifted by God—some of them gifted by God to care for others—and when we take the reins for ourselves, we deny people opportunities to be who they were called to be.

The Ideal Care Minister

An ideal care minister has the following traits:

- a servant's heart;
- active church membership;
- regular worship attendance;
- scriptural and theological foundation, and a willingness to learn;
- knowledge and study of scripture to provide a foundation for care;
- active pursuit of growth in the Christian life;
- is a deeply committed Christian who lives out a life of faith by loving God and other people;
- gives financially in proportion to income with the tithe being the goal;
- Safe Gatherings or other types of certification to assure an understanding of boundaries; and
- is expected to commit to at least three hours per week to this ministry.

Tips for Recruiting your CCMs

1. Pray, pray, pray.
2. Practice discernment.
3. Invite individuals to apply.
4. Establish the application process early.

Questions for Reflection

- What does an ideal CCM look like in your context?
- Who comes to mind when you think of the ideal CCM?
- Develop a plan for recruiting your first class of CCMs.

Notes, Reflections, and Ideas

Essential 2

Define Roles and Responsibilities

The Congregational Care Ministry system works best with three primary collaborative roles: the Director, the CCM, and the Dispatcher. Each of these roles has specific responsibilities and requires certain gifts and skill sets.

Director

Establishes and maintains the Congregational Care Ministry. This is typically a pastor.

Responsibilities: recruitment, training, evaluation, pastoral care for dispather and CCMs
Gifts: vision-casting, organization, care, system-building, discernment

Dispatcher

Connects CCMs to the congregation. The director may serve as the dispatcher. Larger churches may need mulitple dispatchers.

Responsibilities: recieve and process prayer and care requests, assign CCMs to follow up
Gifts: organization, communication, technology skills, discernment

CCM

Provides care on behalf of the congregation. Laity are chosen through application process.

Responsibilities: visitation, calls, one-on-one meetups, care group leadership
Gifts: compassion, empathy, interpersonal warmth, ability to maintain personal boundaries

All CCMs have their own lived experiences that make them uniquely situated to care for people with spe cific circumstances. Some people are relational and are quite capable of making hospital visits, telephone calls, or sitting with people who need encouragement and prayer. Some CCMs have great administrative skills and provide amazing support. Some CCMs may be professionally adept with finances, counseling, or medicine.

Potential Launch Team for a Small to Mid-Sized Church

- Director of Congregational Care, who might also function as the Dispatcher. *receives requests & assigns LCMs*
- Senior Pastor, who functionally serves as a specialist CCM, caring for all funerals and critical care needs.
- Three Congregational Care Ministers, who serve as generalists at first. The more specific the prayer requests become, the more they grow into specialized care.

Questions for Reflection

- Which of the three roles might your new CCMs each fit?
- Are there additional roles necessary in your context?
- What might that look like?
- How will all of the roles collaborate to provide the best care possible?

Notes, Reflections, and Ideas

Essential 3

Establish the Documentation System

Records help maintain institutional and personal memory and provide a transition when pastors change, leave, or are not available. They help avoid "time flies" problems and address claims that you didn't give care to a congregant. Documenting conversations relieves congregants of the pain of retelling a traumatic story repeatedly, and it reminds people that they are cared for and remembered.

Three Steps for Effective Congregational Care

1. Intake and Dispatch
2. Follow-Up *(weekly)*
3. Documentation

Intake and Dispatch

- Audit how your church receives prayer requests. Consider adding prayer request cards in the sanctuary, and digital options on your website and social media pages.

- Keep track of all hospitalizations, deaths, and serious care needs.

- Designate someone to curate and share these care needs with the Dispatcher.

- Dispatcher connects with CCMs to share assignments for the week.

Confidentiality is key! Evaluate how you will best communicate prayer requests with your community. Creating a covenant prayer team is a great way to continue offering prayer on a continual basis while committing to confidentiality.

Weekly Flow Example

Monday: Dispatcher works with the administrative assistant to curate all prayer and care requests. Dispatcher meets with the Director of Congregational Care to assign CCMs. Dispatcher sends email to CCMs with assignments for the week.

Tuesday–Sunday: CCMs read and acknowledge their assignments for the week. They make care calls and visits then document their interactions.

If non-emergent requests for care come **midweek**, via phone or on-line, they are held until the following Monday's curation day. If emergency requests for care come midweek, the Dispatcher and Director discern whether to assign a CCM or a pastor for care. The nature of the emergency determines this decision. If your church has a prayer team, consider how to handle prayer requests midweek.

Questions for Reflection

- Articulate in one sentence how congregants can request care at your church.

- Who receives those requests, and what happens next?

- How will CCMs know what their assignments for the week are?

- Develop a predictable and reliable weekly flow for CCMs to guarantee care.

Follow-Up

Flowchart for CCMs to determine next steps for prayer/care follow-up:

CCM DOCUMENTATION

CCM checks email to find prayer/care assignments for the week on the shared spreadsheet.
Do you see your name for an assignment?

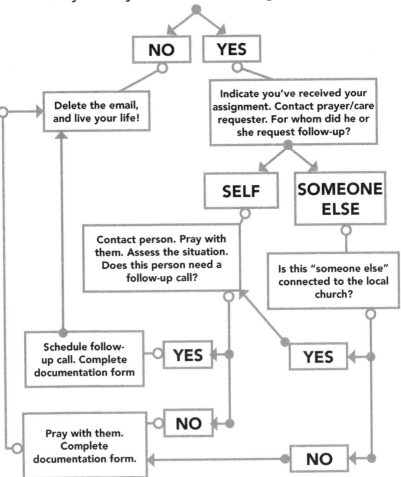

NO

YES

Delete the email, and live your life!

Indicate you've received your assignment. Contact prayer/care requester. For whom did he or she request follow-up?

SELF

SOMEONE ELSE

Contact person. Pray with them. Assess the situation. Does this person need a follow-up call?

Is this "someone else" connected to the local church?

Schedule follow-up call. Complete documentation form

YES

YES

Pray with them. Complete documentation form.

NO

NO

It may feel counterintuitive to follow up with the one requesting prayer rather than the person for whom we are praying, but we must do so in order to do no harm.

Questions for Reflection

- What are the ways that CCMs will follow up?

- What tools will you offer to CCMs so that they feel well equipped to discern how to handle all types of prayer and care requests?

Documentation

What to Document

- Name of congregant
- Date when care was given
- Reason for care
- Type of visit (phone, in person, etc.)
- CCM responsible
- Pastor responsible
- Last time the person was contacted
- Follow-up date if needed
- Other notes

Helpful Documentation Tools

- Paid Subscriptions
  - Shelby
  - Arena
  - Monday.com
  - Slack
- Free Tools
  - Google Drive
  - Paper filing system

As technology progresses, new platforms will emerge with features appropriate to the Congregational Care Ministry documentation system. Continue to be on the lookout for the best way to document the care at your church.

Questions for Reflection

- How will we guarantee confidentiality with documentation?

- Consider usability for CCMs when documenting—what might work best for them?

- How will all information be stored?

Notes, Reflections, and Ideas

Essential 4

Evaluate

You can build a great system that works perfectly for your size and context, and it will have a little give at first. But as your congregation continues to grow in number and volume of care needed, there's only so much stretch. Eventually, the congregation will out-grow the system, or the congregation will grow down to the size of the organizational system.

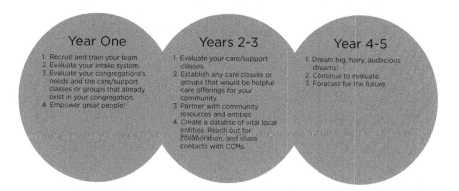

Year One
1. Recruit and train your team.
2. Evaluate your intake system.
3. Evaluate your congregations's needs and the care/support classes or groups that already exist in your congregation.
4. Empower great people!

Years 2-3
1. Evaluate your care/support classes.
2. Establish any care classes or groups that would be helpful care offerings for your community.
3. Partner with community resources and entities.
4. Create a databse of vital local entities. Reach out for collaboration, and share contacts with CCMs.

Year 4-5
1. Dream big, hairy, audacious dreams!
2. Continue to evaluate.
3. Forecast for the future.

Classes and Groups

Group ministry can be very beneficial because common experiences provide empathetic responses and teach others appropriate responses to others' needs. Groups can provide times to teach curriculum to large numbers of people, which can be a time-saving way to minister to people who are facing similar situations.

Tips for Starting a Class or Group

- Start with a three- to five-week class to gauge interest.

- Recruit and train good facilitators, skilled at leading such a group.

- Assist your leaders in choosing or developing their own curriculum with a spiritual component.

- Publicize well.

- Continue to evaluate.

Questions for Reflection

- What are your church's current primary needs?

- What are your community's current primary needs?

- How might your church offer a faith-based response to those communal needs?

- What resources already exist in the community that would be good to share with your CCMs?

- What needs do you anticipate in your church and community in the coming years?

- What care groups already exist? What needs to exist? What needs to be pruned?

- What's your big, hairy, audacious dream for care in your community? What would it take for that to become a reality?

Notes, Reflections, and Ideas

Essential 5

Build the Congregational Need

Buy-in from the congregation is crucial to the development of the Congregational Care Ministry.

Strategic Conversations for Buy-In

Staff/Pastor Parish Relations Committee

This team oversees the work of the pastors and staff. Discuss with them:

- strategic plans for other ministry initiatives,

- hours spent on care each week in relation to other ministry responsibilities,

- hours needed for new initiatives,

- honest evaluation of personal boundaries and Sabbath, and

- presenting the congregational care ministry model as a solution.

Church Council

This team functions as the strategic body of the church, comprising representatives from all existing teams. Discuss with them:

- SPRC's approval for the Congregational Care Ministry model, and

- deep dive into how the ministry will function, along with a reassurance that the pastors continue to provide care alongside CCMs.

Influencers

All churches have those natural leaders whom others respect, even when they do not hold official leadership positions in the church. When you can gain the trust of the church influencers they will publicly support and endorse the ministry. Discuss with such leaders:

- a short overview of plans for the next phases of ministry, including the vision for the Congregational Care Ministry.

Laity to Recruit

Identify leaders who display the gifts necessary to be a CCM. Discuss:

- gifts they display,

- in transparent conversation the need for Congregational Care Ministry, and

- share the vision for the Congregational Care Ministry and invite them to consider applying to be a CCM.

Internal Church Communications

- Cast the vision for the ministry from the official internal communication channels of the church:
  - o Sunday morning bulletins
  - o Weekly eBlasts
  - o Monthly newsletters

From the Pulpit

- **State of the Church Address.** This is much like a town hall meeting for the church. Share information and stories about ministry at the church over the previous year.

- **Sermons.** Use that time to build the need and make heroes out of those who answer God's call to use their gifts!

- **Commissioning Service.** Once your CCMs have been trained, commission them publicly during a worship service in order to affirm their ministry.
  - o Choose a strategic time to commission. Consider when your congregation tends to re-engage and attendance is higher.

Questions for Reflection

- With whom do you need to have conversations?

- Through which channels will you communicate the shift to the Congregational Care Ministry model?

- How will you incorporate building the need into sermons?

- What is your time line?

Notes, Reflections, and Ideas

PART TWO

Congregational Care
Minister's Training Segments

Theology of Care

Jesus traveled throughout Galilee, teaching in their synagogues.
He announced the good news of the kingdom and healed every
disease and sickness among the people.

—Matthew 4:23

Three Key Roles to Consider

Where and how do you see yourself serving in these roles?

prayer
restoration
grace

Prophet
offers redemption and restoration to individuals, relationships, and institutions

Priest
steeped in prayer, offers leadership and guidance through the light, love, and peace of God

Physician
full of grace, evaluates and provides for the needs of the people

The Wesleyan Quadrilateral

Consider how you process any situation through the lens of the Wesleyan Quadrilateral.

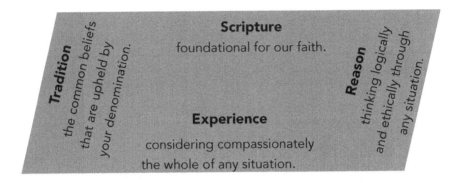

Remember the Three Rules

Questions for Reflection

- How is the Christlike way lived out in your context?
- How would you describe the collective consciousness of your faith community? Is it full of grace, understanding, and welcoming? Do you sense pain or grief that persists?

Notes, Reflections, and Ideas

The most basic tool we have

Segment Two

In All Things, Pray First

Don't be anxious about anything; rather, bring up all of your requests to God in your prayers and petitions, along with giving thanks. Then the peace of God that exceeds all understanding will keep your hearts and minds safe in Christ Jesus.

—Philippians 4:6-7

Prayer lifts us up and out of the chaos of the moment to a different reality. That reality is where we connect with God and where restoration can happen.

—Rev. Karen Lampe

Common Forms of Prayer

It is helpful to memorize a few simple frameworks for prayer, which you can call upon whenever then need arises. The ACTS form of prayer is a multisubject prayer model. It has an informal feel, and is a common method for praying aloud.

ACTS
1. Adoration
2. Confession
3. Thanksgiving
4. Supplication (the "ask")

The Collect

[handwritten: always and in everything, God's will be done]

The Collect is a one-subject prayer and typically has a somewhat formal feel. The words and phrases flow into a more poetic form and often focus on one subject such as illness, seeking peace, recovery, and so on. The Book of Common Prayer is an excellent resource for this method of prayer.

THE COLLECT *[handwritten: the Book of Common Prayer]*
1. Invocation (calling out to God)
2. Attribute of God (Prince of Peace, Counselor, Healer)
3. Petition (requests)
4. Purpose ("so that" . . . anticipated result)
5. Closing (in Jesus's name)
6. Affirmation (Amen. Let it be so.)

Praying Scripture

Read a scripture slowly aloud several times, emphasizing different words or phrases with each reading.

PRAYING SCRIPTURE

1. Read a scripture aloud.
2. Contemplate the scripture.
3. Utilize the words in your prayer.

WRITING EXTEMPORANEOUS PRAYERS

1. Cathartic action to connect with God
2. Preparing ourselves for next steps
3. Centering ourselves
4. Writing out what is on our hearts

Utilizing Prayer Corporately in Church

1. Evaluate how your prayer requests are currently being received and responded to in your church.

2. Are there corporate prayer traditions and vigils in your church? Are they effective?

3. Do you have spaces (inside or out-of-doors) that draw people to prayer?

Making Time for Self-Care

"Peace I leave with you. My peace I give you."

—John 14:27a

1. What is your daily prayer routine and discipline?

2. What does it mean to pray without ceasing?

Practice Time!

- If you are in a group, spend time praying for one another.

- If you are alone, take time to do a breath prayer, praying over a scripture or writing your prayers down in a journal.

Questions for Reflection

- How could your community benefit from an increased focus on prayer?

- Who are the champions on your team for this effort?

Notes, Reflections, and Ideas

Boundaries

Carry each other's burdens and so you will fulfill the law of Christ.

—Galatians 6:2

Boundaries are the limits or borders we place on relationships that allow us to balance closeness and freedom. Boundaries can exist to safeguard as well as to delineate what is acceptable and unacceptable behavior. When you are ministering to another person, not only do you need to respect their boundaries, you must also set boundaries for your relationship with them. Remember as a pastor or CCM, you are legally considered to be the person of authority, which means you must consider every interaction.

Key Ideas to Consider and Discuss with Your Team

- Be aware of your emotions.

- Be cautious about sharing your personal information.

- Don't share about yourself because you feel the need to talk.

- Only share information if it would be helpful for encouragement or as a teaching example.

- Seek care, counsel, and support for yourself.

- Be aware of your emotional responses/reactions. Do you have emotional triggers?

- Be aware of your actions. Seek feedback from your team members regarding touch and your tone of voice.

Consider These Basic Rules for Good Boundaries

- Never allow yourself to be in an unsafe or compromising situation. Make sure windows have been installed in the doors of rooms used for meeting with congregants. Never care for someone alone in your church.

- Understand that you are in a position of authority when you are caring for someone.

- Never set a "date" for a meal or coffee or travel with a person of the opposite sex for whom you are caring.

- Never go to a home visit alone if it may put you in a dangerous situation.

- Have you taken a course that teaches clear ethical boundaries set by your denomination?

- Do you have clear understanding of clothing for certain situations such as hospital calls?

- Have you ever felt sexual feelings for a congregant, staff member, colleague, or volunteer? Do not put yourself in a vulnerable position. Debrief with someone safe and keep your feelings in check.

- It is never appropriate to be in a romantic relationship with a person for whom you are caring.

- Never share a person's personal information.

- HIPAA protects the privacy of a person's health information. Churches are exempt from HIPAA, but as caregivers, you must diligently guard the confidentiality of your congregations.

Practice

Work in threes to role-play setting safe boundaries. One person will be the caregiver, another person is seeking care, and the third person is the observer.

Possible scenarios:

- a pregnant college-aged student

- an angry wife who is living in an abusive relationship

- a young person unemployed and depressed

- a father or mother of three young children who was just diagnosed with cancer

- a young person whose mother died tragically

Thoughtful Observation

Using the guidelines for boundaries, thoughtfully observe one another as you practice the scenarios. Watch for heightened emotion, the tone of voices, the use of touch, the effect on the caregiver, and the risk to the caregiver.

- How did the caregiver set boundaries?

- How did the person seeking care react to boundaries?

- When were the boundaries pushed or breached? How did the caregiver react?

- How did the caregiver manage the strong emotional atmosphere? If there is time, change roles and repeat this training.

Questions for Reflection

- Whom would you contact regarding ethical issues?

- Do you understand the legalities of pastoral responsibility?

- How will you establish clear pastoral boundaries? How will you communicate to a congregant what those boundaries are?

- How will you maintain personal space during appointments?

- What types of behaviors must be reported to the church or law enforcement? What steps should you take to make a report?

- Have you ever used a personal counselor during especially stressful seasons?

Conclusion

Key to a healing ministry is an understanding of appropriate boundaries that models a deep sense of respect for our care receiver as we help provide a greater connection to God. Developing good boundaries includes:

- being *aware* of your emotions and role as the pastor/CCM;

- observing *caution* in sharing personal information;

- *considering* carefully touch, posture, and tone of voice;

- *understanding* place and time to do visits;

- considering the importance of *confidentiality* while maintaining documentation and debriefing;

- *listening, reflecting, comforting*, and *supporting* with spiritual guidance; and

- practicing *extra caution* with critical situations.

Notes, Reflections, and Ideas

Segment Four

Listening and Spiritual Guidance

Know this, my dear brothers and sisters: everyone should be quick to listen, slow to speak, and slow to grow angry.

—James 1:19

> Many times, people in crisis will come first to their CCM or pastor because they hope to have a safe, confidential place to navigate a difficult situation. Remember that as you take on this role, no one is expecting you to be their savior.

Basic Guidelines for Listening

1. Pray before each conversation.

2. Your body language should convey a nonjudgmental curiosity.

3. Your tone of voice should convey a non-anxious presence.

4. Assure the person of confidentiality.

5. Have them fill out any necessary paperwork that would be good for your records.

6. Convey to them that you'd like to take a few notes.

7. Inform them of your boundaries, such as how many times you will meet.

8. Let them know you are asking as their Congregational Care Minister and that you are not a counselor. You want to offer them spiritual guidance and assurance.

9. Make the space holy if you can. Even if it is a Zoom Room.

10. Pray with the congregant.

11. Be prepared with good clarifying, spiritual questions.

12. Watch for signs of mental health needs such as depression or anxiety.

13. Be empathetic. Allow them to express their emotions.

14. Reflect to them what you have heard.

15. Offer resources such as scripture, books, support group options, online sermons, or classes.

16. Give them homework that will encourage them.

The following paperwork will aid and help you remember these steps.

Permission for Referral

At (name of church) _____, congregational care is guided by a team of counselors, pastors, care coordinators, and others to meet the spiritual, emotional, physical, and relational needs in our lives. At times, it may be necessary to share this background from my client file to most effectively assess, direct, and carry out this holistic care. Likewise, multiple members of the care team may interact with me and collaborate in the caring process.

By signing this form, I give the undersigned pastor(s) permission to present my case file to the staff members of (name of church)_____'s congregational care team and the senior pastor's office when necessary for the advancement of my care. If this pastor does refer me to a resource in the community, this authorization also allows others to follow up with me via email or phone within sixty days to receive feedback regarding that referral. I understand that these decisions will be made in an ethical and responsible manner. In order to honor my time and the pastor's time, each appointment will be limited to one hour.

Client

_____

(signature)   (printed name)   (date)

Client

_____

(signature)   (printed name)   (date)

Pastor

_____

(signature)   (printed name)   (date)

Pastor

_____

(signature)   (printed name)   (date)

FAMILY CONTACT INFORMATION FORM

Your Contact Information

Name	Home Phone
Address	Work Phone
City/State/Zip	Mobile Phone
Email Address	

Family Members

Name	Age	Relationship

Emergency Contact Information

Name	Home Phone
Address	Work Phone
City/State/Zip	Mobile Phone
Email Address	

This Safety and Self-Care Contract can be very helpful in situations of crisis. Never refrain from getting more help by calling in a colleague, pastor, or in extreme cases 911.

SAFETY AND SELF-CARE CONTRACT

I, _____, commit to work toward my own health and safety and the health and safety of others. If I feel as though I might harm myself or someone else, I agree to follow the action steps listed below and ask for help.

I will call one or more of the following people to discuss my feelings:

I will do one or more of the following things to help me manage difficult feelings:

I will seek additional support in one or more of the following ways:

Today I met with

(Pastor)_____

(signature)   *(printed name)*   *(date)*

My signature below indicates that I am refusing emergency assistance, and I am well enough to leave the church of my own accord.

_____

(signature)   *(printed name)*   *(date)*

Emergency 911

National Suicide Prevention Helpline 1-800-273-8255

Church or Pastor _____

Local hospital _____

The Pastoral Care Notes can be a standard form to help you remember important details of your conversations.

PASTORAL CARE NOTES

Member's name:

_____

Date: _____

❑ discussion by phone

❑ discussion in person

Persons present:

_____

Personal history:

_____

Concerns:

_____

_____

Biblical passages/other care offered:

_____

Danger signs (suicide attempts, abuse, etc.):

_____

Referrals:

_____

_____

_____

History of Care

Name:

_____

Visit date:

_____

Visited by:

_____

Details:

_____

_____

_____

Suggested follow-up:

_____

_____

_____

CCM and pastor:

_____

Care plan:

_____

_____

_____

_____

_____

_____

_____

CONGREGATIONAL CARE MEMBER FILE CONTACT LOG

Member Name: _____

Date File Established: _____

DATE	CONGREGATIONAL CARE TEAM MEMBER	PURPOSE

Spiritual Care Assessment

The Spiritual Care Assessment on the following two pages is an excellent tool to use with someone as you help them navigate a challenging life situation. You might encourage them to take a few days to think through the questions and checklist, and then offer them time to work through their ideas with you. This thoughtful process may take two or three sessions with the individual.

SPIRITUAL CARE ASSESSMENT

SUBJECTIVE MEANING OF SITUATION

What does it mean for you that you are in this situation?

How do you make sense of what has happened?

What kinds of things are you learning from all this?

How has the life of the individual changed as a result of the illness/situation?

How do you make sense of or understand the illness/situation?

What purpose or meaning do you give to the life of the individual?

What are your regrets or unresolved needs of forgiveness?

RELATION TO SUPPORT SYSTEM

How do you think your family is doing with this situation?

What group or organization is important for providing support?

What network will be available at home?

What are the individual/family regrets or unresolved needs of forgiveness?

CONCEPT OF GOD

Where is (or, do you see) God in all this?

APPROACH TO HOPE

What are your hopes?

What are your fears?

What does having hope mean for you at this time?

How have you kept a sense of hope in the past?

What has gotten you through difficult times in the past?

What helps the individual/family get through tough times like this?

With the time you have left, what are your prayers and hopes?

Pastor's signature: _____Date:_____

Spiritual Care Checklist

Spiritual Issues Presented by Individual and Support System

❏ Guilt/forgiveness	❏ Hopelessness	❏ Terminal condition
❏ Regrets	❏ Helplessness	❏ Peace
❏ Conflict with values/beliefs	❏ Concerns about relationship with God	❏ Concerns with meaning/purpose
❏ Grief	❏ Conflict with faith	❏ Change or loss
❏ Concerns about afterlife	❏ Thanksgiving	❏ Loss of support community
❏ Fear of suffering	❏ Anxiety	❏ Difficult decisions
❏ Hope	❏ Ethical decisions	❏ Financial concerns
❏ Fear of death	❏ Interpersonal conflict	❏ Other

Please provide a brief explanation about the checks made above:

Spiritual Components of Spiritual Care Plan/Intervention

❏ No concern	❏ Spiritual concern	❏ Spiritual distress	❏ Spiritual despair

❏ Ethical concerns	❏ Spiritual support	❏ Referred ritual request
❏ Expression/validation of feelings	❏ Prayer	❏ Referral
❏ Collaboration with clergy	❏ Grief support	❏ Communication
❏ Notify personal clergy	❏ Expression/validation of beliefs	❏ Facilitate coping
❏ Family support	❏ Caring presence	❏ Rite/ritual
❏ Ongoing support		

❏ Sets realistic goals	❏ Reduced guilt	❏ Demonstrates ability to cope
❏ Declined visit	❏ Reports sense of forgiveness	❏ Reports reconciliation with others or God
❏ Reports less spiritual distress	❏ Uses faith in coping	❏ Uses personal values in decision making
❏ Reports less emotional distress	❏ Reports renewed sense of purpose	❏ Participates in decisions
❏ Renewed sense of peace	❏ Demonstrates reduced anxiety	❏ Reports sense of control/independence
❏ Renewed hope	❏ Uses personal spiritual resources	❏ Uses support system

Please provide a brief explanation about the checks made above:

Four Practice Care Scenarios

One key way to prepare for difficult situations is to practice with your team. Take time to role-play these care scenarios to help you prepare for situations you might face.

Care Scenario 1

You've been assigned to a congregant who has recently gone through a very difficult divorce, has a small child, and is experiencing financial difficulty. She has reached out for financial assistance from the church and was not happy with the result. She feels the church has let her down. You have met with her a couple of times to encourage her and pray with her. She starts calling you often, at times more than once a day and expects you to be available immediately. She's frantic for help and for someone to listen to her. How can you best support her in your role as a CCM?

Care Scenario 2

You have been asked to reach out to a man who lost his job. His wife put in a prayer request and has explained her husband is agreeable to meeting with someone. You have called and left a phone message and sent an e-mail. He has not responded to your call or e-mail in two days. You phone him and leave another message. You do not hear back. What do you do?

Care Scenario 3

You are participating in a class that has been meeting for a few weeks. A new person joins the class and begins to share his tragic story. He explains he is needing support but is trusting in God to provide. He then shares a theological opinion that doesn't go over well with a majority of the group. People become argumentative and open their Bibles to point to scripture to counter what he's saying. They are really in attack mode. You sense the man is very distraught and angry. What do you do?

Care Scenario 4

You met with a woman for the first time and she shared with you she is living with a husband who abuses her. She shares she is a devout Christian and can't possibly leave her husband because of the covenant she made and the scriptures she's read that tell her she must remain a loyal and dedicated wife. What do you do? How can you shift her thinking from feeling oppressed or victimized to confident and capable?

Questions for Reflection

- Whom do you consider to be a good listener? Why?

- What is your prayer routine before, during, and after meeting with someone seeking care?

- Using the listening guidelines, evaluate your listening skills. What is working well? What needs improvement?

Notes, Reflections, and Ideas

Visitation: The Most Sacred Hours

If any of you are suffering, they should pray.

—James 5:13

> In normal times, barring pandemics or natural disasters, in person "visitation" is one of the most important elements of care that can be offered through the church. Yet we must be nimble and adapt to challenges so that visitation can continue in different forms as needed. All the more reason to remember this is a team effort!

Whether a person is hospitalized, home bound, in a rehab center or long-term care, visitation is a sacred holy ministry. With each person you visit, take time before to pray so you are guided by the Holy Spirit to understand more fully the complexity of their situation. Remember, too, that there is opportunity to care not just for the suffering person but also their family and friends. Compassionate care is a great gift to give—and to receive.

As a team, go over your shared protocols and boundaries concerning visitation. This will help all of you to work effectively to provide continuity of care.

Local Church's Protocol to Receive Information

1. Provide information to one central triage person.

2. Provide pager or important phone numbers.

3. Provide pastor's info.

4. Keep a list of local hospital numbers and addresses.

5. Website link to receive information.

6. Other?

Key Guidelines for Visitation

- Wear washable clothing.

- Wear a name tag.

- Keep clean masks readily available (car, home, etc.).

- Carry a Bible, anointing oil, and business cards.

- Perhaps carry a small supply of appropriate gifts in your car.

- Have a list of key scriptures written down.

- Consider keeping this *Manual* handy, perhaps in your car, for quick reference.

Key Guidelines and Resources during Pandemic and Natural Disasters

- Do not visit if you are sick.

- Do not go alone if there is any obvious danger.

- Adapt technologically to the situation.

- Keep clean masks, gloves, and other appropriate clothing available.

- Observe other important local guidelines.

Key Guidelines for the Frail and Elderly

- Know the names of key nursing facilities.

- Remember the names of key staff.

- Learn the names of key care receivers.

- Observe the local protocol for a pandemic or other special circumstances.

- Speak and move slowly.

- Always wear your name tag; also always tell the person your name.

- Kneel or sit in a chair at eye level.

- Do not hurry.

- Allow them time to tell their stories.

- Be ready with anointing oil, scripture, prayer and communion if allowed.

Key Guidelines for Documentation in Your Local Church

Basic documentation instructions include:

1. Hospital visitation schedule with important contact information.

2. Assignment of CCMs to each person to provide for continuity of care.

3. Notes about the visit kept either electronically or in a shared confidential written form.

4. Keep the pastor informed.

Key Local Resources Info (Addresses and Phone Numbers)

Keep a list of the following resource information in cases where persons need more help than you are able to provide:

- hospitals,

- care homes,

- food pantries,

- mental health agencies, and

- other important resources.

Questions for Reflection

- What is your protocol for visiting people in the hospital in normal times as well as during times of social distancing? What about pre-surgery calls?

- What is your protocol for care extended to someone who may be in quarantine or hospitalized for highly infectious disease?

- What communication channels are available to alert you to a person who seeks care in the hospital, rehabilitation facility, or care home?

Medical Terminology

Head

Gamma Knife: A device that delivers a high-radiation dose of gamma rays to small areas within the head for tumors or vascular abnormalities. It requires a halo attached to the skull so the dose is delivered very accurately. The machine has been adapted for wider use, and is called a CyberKnife System and can even be used for radiating parts that move, for example, the lung.

Dura: The sack in which the brain floats.

Epidural: Outside or above the dura. In cases of bleeding, indicates where the blood is collecting. Epidural is the most dangerous type of bleeding, as the bleeding is usually arterial.

Subdural: Under the dura. Usually venous bleeding and is at a slower rate so it does not cause great damage and many times will resolve without surgery.

Burr holes: Holes drilled in the skull to relieve pressure in the brain.

Strokes, thrombotic vs. embolic: A thrombotic clot forms in a damaged vessel and causes it to shut off blood supply and hence causes a stroke. An embolic clot is formed elsewhere, usually in the heart, and it gets into the arteries to goes the head and blocks a vessel.

Strokes, red vs. white: A white stroke causes the brain to be blanched in color as the blood has been shut off by the blockage. As this happens, the supportive tissue for the brain begins to collapse, and with that bleeding occurs into the brain where the stroke is, which turns the brain red.

Ventricles: Fluid-filled spaces in the brain where spinal fluid is manufactured.

Lumbar puncture: A procedure to remove fluid, to lower pressure in the head, or to collect samples for cultures or to diagnose malignancies.

Diagnostic procedures: CT scan, MRI, and so on.

Aneurysms: Weak spots in vessels that leak and cause strokes.

Shunts: Devices placed in the brain to relieve brain pressure secondary to spinal fluid. The shunts are low-pressure devices that siphon the fluid away and route it into the chest or abdominal cavity via a catheter inserted under the skin.

Epidural anesthesia and injections: Medicine or anesthesia placed in the epidural space, the space around the spinal cord. The cord is also surrounded by dura.

ENT: Ear-Nose-Throat

Nose-packing: Anterior, front of the nose, easy to do and remove; posterior, hard to place and hard to remove, and very uncomfortable for the patient. Used with nosebleeds and sinus and nasal surgery.

Chest

Pleurisy: Inflammation of the pleura, the lining of the chest cavity and the covering on the lungs.

Effusions: Collections of fluid within a cavity, chest, or abdomen.

Chest tubes: Tubes placed in the chest to drain fluid or to reinflate a lung.

CPAP and PEEP: Ways of ventilating a patient to enhance breathing, support breathing, or push fluid out of the lungs. CPAP, Continuous Positive Airway Pressure; PEEP, Positive End Expiratory Pressure.

Vents: Automatic devices to control the patient's breathing. Requires an endotracheal tube or a tracheostomy.

Flow meters: Devices to make patient breathe better after surgery to prevent pneumonia.

Bronchoscopy: Procedure to look into the airways for biopsy or collection of samples of lung fluids, sputum.

Thoracentesis: Draining fluid from the chest cavity with a needle, usually to get samples for cancer screening or cultures.

Heart

Echocardiogram (EKG), ejection fractions: Using sound waves, physicians can learn about the functions and size of the heart and get ideas about how the pump works and make an estimation of how effective the heart is working. The ejection fraction is a percent measure of how much of the blood that is pushed into a ventricle gets pushed out with each contraction; it should be above 50 percent.

Cardiac catheterization and stents: The catheterization is a diagnostic procedure used to look at the heart from the inside. Pressure within the chambers can be measured. Xrays with dye injections can be taken to evaluate the potency of the vessels. Those narrowed can usually be opened with stents—small, metal, screenlike tubes placed within the narrowed arteries.

Pacemakers: Electronic devices installed to correct and control heart rate problems.

Pacemaker/Defibrillator units: Pacemakers can also shock the heart with electricity to stop rhythms like ventricular tachycardia or ventricular fibrillation, both dangerous rhythms that can lead to cardiac arrest and sudden death.

CABG: Coronary Artery Bypass Graft: A surgery used to bypass areas of blockage in the coronary arteries. It is beginning to be done again as the treatment of choice for blockage instead of stenting.

Balloon pump: A temporary device used to help a sick heart pump better. The balloon is placed in the left ventricle to take up space so the injured heart does not have to work so hard to pump the blood out. The pump does the pushing and allows the heart to rest a bit.

VAD: Ventricular Assist Device: An external pump more permanent than the balloon, which can be used when the patient is waiting for a transplant.

Monitoring: Each of the blips on an EKG has a letter assigned to it.

VPCs: Ventricular Premature Contractions are extra-big beats, which feels like the heart has slammed into the inside of the chest wall. Generally means very little, but can be annoying. Too may VCPs too close together can cause bad ventricular rhythms to develop.

DVT: Deep vein thrombosis is a blood clot in one's lower extremity. Preventions include aspirin, blood thinners, early mobility of the patient, and compression stockings, all to prevent pulmonary emboli, clots thrown into the lungs.

CHF: Congestive heart failure, secondary to many causes. The injured organ cannot handle the volume of blood and fluid in it and everything begins to back up. The heart increases in size and the flabby muscle tries to keep up. Fluid collects in the lungs, the liver swells, and the lower extremities are filled with fluid. Treatments are directed at fluid removal and medications to get the heart to pump better. Rotating tourniquets can be placed on all four extremities to diminish the blood return to the heart so it can better handle the smaller amount.

Pulse oximetry: The red blinking finger tool, which is the easiest way to measure the concentration of oxygen in the blood.

Measuring Arterial blood gases: Drawing blood from an artery and measuring the concentration of oxygen and carbon dioxide in the blood. Much more accurate and very useful for people on ventilation devices.

Event monitors: Portable devices to record cardiac activity. The patient wears this and when she or he feels something unusual going on with the heart, she or he turns it on and records the event. The recordings are read by the cardiologist. Holter monitoring is also done, in which the device is on all the time and the recordings are made for a fixed amount of time and used to diagnose rhythm problems.

Cardioversion: Convert heart rhythm to normal with electroshock. This takes place in a cath lab, commonly done to convert atrial rhythm abnormalities like atrial fibrillation and atrial flutter.

Physiologic mapping: A way to map out the normal electric circuits within the heart, and find abnormal ones to treat rhythm abnormalities. Ablation procedures and electrical destruction are performed to get rid of abnormal circuits, which can produce troublesome rhythm disorders.

Aneurysm: An aortic aneurysm, a weak spot in the great vessel, that can blow out and cause instant death. In many cases it can be treated with a stent, but is commonly treated with open-heart surgery when a graft for the damaged portion is installed.

Infectious Disease

C difficile: A diarrhea-producing organism.

Coronavirus: A type of virus that can infect your nose, sinuses, and upper throat.

COVID-19: A type of coronavirus that will cause mild to moderate symptoms in most people but can cause severe acute respiratory symptoms as well as affect other organ systems. Be sure to follow and understand the safety protocol provided by national and local authorities.

MRSA: Methicillin-resistant Staphylococcus aureus infection. Any patient with MRSA should be your last visit of the day. Don't visit anyone after you visit him or her.

VRE: Vancomycin resistant enterococcus. Common denominators in all these organisms make the patient very sick, leaving him or her in the hospital for long periods time, receiving massive amounts of antibiotics. These bugs have largely become resistant to antibiotics, making treatment very difficult.

PICC lines: Peripherally inserted central catheter, used for medications that are very irritating to peripheral veins, and also for feeding patients nutritional supplements intravenously when they cannot swallow.

Gastrointestinal

EGD: Esophagogastroduodenoscopy is a procedure to look into the stomach and first portion of the small bowel with a scope.

ERCP: Endoscopic retrograde cholangiopancreatography is a procedure to look into the ductwork of the liver, pancreas, and gallbladder. Generally done with complicated gallstone patients, and those with a probable diagnosis of cancer, especially pancreatic.

Feeding tubes: Tubes placed through the stomach wall for those who will have long-term issues with nutrition.

Hyperalimentation parenteral (IV) nutrition: A way of feeding a patient nutritional fluids through a vein.

NG tubes: Nasogastric tubes. Usually used post-op to keep fluids from accumulating in the stomach. Also used in bowel obstructions to allow the bowel to rest.

Ascites: An effusion in the abdomen, a collection of fluid.

Peracentesis: Removal of abdominal fluid with a needle, for diagnosis or patient comfort.

Stents: Can also be placed in the pancreatic duct to treat those who have repeating bouts of acute pancreatitis.

Liver biopsy: To remove a piece of the liver through a special needle for diagnostic reasons.

GI camera: A very small camera swallowed within a capsule. It actually takes pictures of the entire GI tract, many areas not seen by any other means, and transmits the pictures to a recording device worn by the patient. The recording device is connected to a computer to look at the images.

Genitourinary Creatinine: A chemical measured that indicates urinary flow and rate of kidney functioning.

BPH: Benign Prostatic Hypertrophy.

Laser: The use of a laser light to destroy excess prostate that has become a problem.

Kidney biopsy: Taking a piece of a kidney for diagnostic reasons. It usually requires a trip to the ultrasound room to have the tech mark the kidneys' location on the patient's back for the doctor who will be taking the biopsy. A possible problem post-biopsy is bleeding.

Back and Neck Ortho

Fusions: Joints in the spine are made solid by adding bone from a cadaver or from the patient himself or herself, so those joints do not move anymore. This is done primarily for pain relief. Any joint in the body can be made solid by fusion.

Rods, cages: Other ways to make the lower back and the neck more solid to relieve pain from arthritic or disc-related problems.

Fracture: A broken bone.

PT/ Rehab: Physical therapy designed to get the patient moving again. Not uncommon after most orthopedic procedures, especially joint replacements.

OT: Occupational therapy, teaching patients activities of daily living so they are able to take care of their own needs when they are sent home.

Transplants/Hematology

Laminar flow rooms and floors: Positive pressure areas in hospitals, on chemo units, and in operating rooms where the air pressure inside the rooms is greater than the air pressure outside the room. This keeps less-sterilized air from the outside from moving into the pressurized areas, to keep that air cleaner and protect the patients from risks of infections.

Isolation procedures, hand washing before and after, and sanitizer: Important for all visits, but absolutely necessary in laminar flow areas. Frequently you will pass through an air lock, a small room where there will be the first chance to wash your hands.

Tissue rejection in transplants: This happens in all transplant patients, and is generally treated well and suppressed with antirejection medications. Despite donor matching, our bodies still recognize the new parts as foreign material and try to destroy them.

Graft versus host reactions: Another kind of rejection process, but one in which the graft tries to destroy the host. The graft can also recognize the host as foreign material and will attempt to destroy it, and it can. Usually much more difficult to treat and control and the results can be devastating, with major portions of the body of the recipient being involved and ultimately destroyed.

Bone marrow biopsy: A procedure to obtain bone marrow for diagnosis and also as a way of looking at response to treatments. Usually taken from the crest of the hipbone. Can also use the sternum, and in kids, the large bone of the lower extremity. Sedation is needed, as this is a very painful procedure.

Auto-transfusion: Banking your own blood and then using it if needed when you have surgery.

Cancer Staging

In situ stage: Cancer totally confined to one spot.

I, II, III, IV stages: The different kinds of cancer and the organ from which it came will dictate how the staging is indicated. Generally:

Stage I: Very little local invasion.

Stage II: A little more local invasion with a few close nodes involved.

Stage III: Wider local invasion, increased size to the primary growth and spread to lymph nodes that are at a distance.

Stage IV: More of stage III but the tumor has also spread to involve other organs nearby or at a distance. Can involve any organ.

Positron Emission Tomography (PET) scans: The best test to define where the cancer is. Red blood cells are taken from the patient. They are tagged with radioactive sugar and then put back into the patient. After a time, the scan is completed. Because cancer cells are rapidly replicating, they tend to pick up the radioactive sugar and light up on the scans. This allows one to see where the cancer is spreading. The scan can also be used to look at response to treatments as well.

Portacaths: A device installed under the skin through which chemotherapy is given. Chemo is very irritating to the veins and must be given through this central catheter to protect the smaller veins in the arms and hands. These units can be left in for long times with the biggest risk of infection being in the port itself. In such cases it has to be replaced or removed.

Other

Bedrail alarms: Most all beds in hospitals are alarmed. They will emit a chirp when a person leans on them and then with significant pressure will really wail. They warn people to stay away from them.

Chair alarms: A pressure pad that does nothing as long as one stays sitting on it. If a person moves off it, it will sound a loud alarm.

Restraints: Devices used to keep patients in their beds. It may appear cruel, but it is better than more injury from falls. Sometimes, these devices include heavy mittens, which are used to protect the visitor and the staff.

Notes, Reflections, and Ideas

Leading through the Darkest Valley

Even when I walk through the darkest valley,
I fear no danger because you are with me.

—Psalm 23:4

Care for the dying is one of the greatest services that we can provide as pastors and CCMs. It can feel daunting if one tries to do this type of care alone, so again, a team effort allows for more connections with the family and friends.

It is important to prepare and inform your congregation through sermon, website, and small groups about the dying process and what to expect from the church throughout this part of their life's journey. Let them know that you are committed to them and their loved ones. Continuity of care is particularly important during this time so that the patient and family know that the assigned CCM and pastor understand their situation.

During a time of social distancing, the dying process can feel especially lonely and incomplete as our usual traditional methods of care are not possible. As caregivers we must rely on our team to communicate more intently so that the family and congregant are assured of God's presence throughout.

One helpful tool to offer is a spiritual autobiography. Below you will see what a typical document of this type could include. Some people will use this to an even greater extent, creating more personal statements for their closest family members. Other people will not be as eager to work on the document as it might seem daunting or an unwanted reminder of their mortality.

Scriptures

Take time to choose the appropriate scriptures for your visits. Certain passages are particularly helpful throughout the dying process. You may want to ask the person about their favorite verses of scripture and what particularly speaks to them in the passage. You may want to follow up your visit with a handwritten note with the scripture that was read. After the visit, document what scriptures were used and any conversation that may help you or other care team members with the next visit. Below is a list that is not exhaustive but will help you begin to develop your own favorites scriptures for visitation.

Psalm 23	Matthew 6:9-13
Psalm 46	John 14:1-6a, 18-19, 25-27
Psalm 69	Romans 8:38-39
Psalm 86	1 Corinthians 15:42-57
Psalm 91	2 Corinthians 4:8-18
Psalm 100	2 Corinthians 5:1-7
Psalm 116	Philippians 4:4-7
Psalm 138	Revelation 21:1-5
Isaiah 43:1-5	

SPIRITUAL AUTOBIOGRAPHY

Name:

_____

Date: _____

What is your first memory of church?

_____
_____
_____
_____
_____

What church has been most foundational in your life? Why?

_____
_____
_____
_____
_____

Were you baptized? Describe that experience.

_____
_____
_____
_____
_____

When did you attend our church for the first time? Describe that first day.

_____
_____
_____
_____
_____

Describe the connections you have made within the church. Why are they important?

_____

_____

_____

_____

What are your three favorite scriptures? Why are these significant to you? What do they say about your life?

1. _____

_____

_____

2. _____

_____

_____

3. _____

_____

_____

What are your three favorite hymns/faith songs? Why?

1. _____

_____

_____

2. _____

_____

_____

3. _____

_____

_____

Do you have daily spiritual practices? If so, what are they?

_____

_____

_____

_____

What is the most important thing you have done in your life?

_____
_____
_____
_____
_____
_____

What is your legacy?

_____
_____
_____
_____
_____

At the end of your life celebration, what are the three most important things that people hear about you?

1. _____
_____
_____

2. _____
_____
_____

3. _____
_____
_____

Miscellaneous:

_____
_____
_____
_____
_____

Prayer

Perhaps now more than ever, your prayers will bring comfort and assurance to the suffering as well as the family. Always ask if you can offer prayer and what they would like you to pray for. Initially, when a person receives a serious diagnosis you may be praying for a cure, a modern miracle, the best medical care, and increased strength. Before your visits, pray for yourself to be a nonanxious presence that exudes the peace, love, light, and grace of Christ.

As the journey begins, prayers should focus on patience, assurance, continued guidance from the medical caregivers, and increased calm. An example of such a prayer would be:

Loving, healing God, we come to you with gratitude, knowing that you are walking with (name) and his/her family. Lord, as (name) has just received this diagnosis, we know you want the very best for (name), so we ask that you bring the very best of medical care to her/him that he/she might receive a modern miracle. Help (name) to release the fear and anxiety that he/she maybe feeling. With each breath, allow him/her to breathe in your peace, light, and love. Help (name) and his/her family experience your holy hand providing them with new strength and peace. Help us as a church family to care for him/her as he/she walks this journey. All this we pray in the healing name of Jesus. Amen.

As the condition of the patient deteriorates, your prayers will evolve to accommodate the health challenges as well as the person's spiritual and mental wellbeing. The patient may ask for specific prayers for their family members or any unfinished business that maybe concerning them. An example of such a prayer maybe:

Gracious Loving God, we come to you today thankful for your continued presence and help as (name) continues to struggle with pain and weakness. We know that this can be a fearful time for (name) and his/her family. We ask that you bless (name) especially with new strength and assurance of your presence that (name)'s days will have a greater connection to you as well as his/her family. Bring to (name) and his/her family a peace that passes understanding as he/she shares these sacred moments. All this we pray in the name of our great comforter Jesus. Amen.

As the journey draws to a close, prayers could shift more to comfort, assurances of eternal life, and peace. Watch for moments when you can offer prayer with family members and friends who may be struggling with the pending death. Allow them time to express their worries and fears about death. This is an amazing time as a CCM or pastor to share your own beliefs. If the person dying is nonresponsive during a visit, continue to talk to them as well as read scripture and anoint. Another wonderful blessing is to sing to them or have someone else come sing to them. They may not be able to respond but may still be hearing everything.

Such a prayer at this stage may include:

Merciful Lord of light and love, we are so grateful for your presence in this holy space with (name). In the quiet of this room, bring to them a sense of divine peace that passes understanding. Bring to them assurance for their family and friends that you will be guiding them. Release them from their pain in your perfect timing that they may dance in your presence in their new spiritual body. All this we pray in the name of him who still teaches us to pray: Our Father, who art in heaven. Hallowed be thy name. Thy kingdom come, thy will be done on earth as it is heaven. Give us this day our daily bread and forgive us our trespasses as we forgive those who trespass against us. And lead us not into temptation, but deliver us from evil, for thine is the kingdom and the power and the glory forever. Amen.

Scriptures at the Time of Death

When death is imminent, scriptures to use at the bedside or on a socially distanced phone call (or using other technology) include:

2 Corinthians 4:7-18; 5:1-7
> These verses are especially helpful before death to help the dying person as well as their family, assuring them that this earthly body is temporary, but we have a new spiritual body after this life.

Revelation 21:1-5
> This passage assures us that God is making all things new and that we are being readied to be "born" into eternity.

1 Corinthians 15:44, 50-57
> This scripture passage assures the dying that our new eternal body is awaiting us and that death will not have the last word because Christ has given us the victory over death.

John 14:1-6a, 18-19, 27-28
> This passage especially helps the dying as well as those gathered release their fears and experience the sacred peace of Christ.

Romans 8:38-39
> This passage affirms that nothing—not even death—can separate us from the love of God in Christ Jesus our Lord.

Psalm 23 or the Lord's Prayer
> After you offer prayer, either the Twenty-Third Psalm or the Lord's Prayer adds an element of peace.

After Death Has Occurred

- Continue to be a non-anxious presence that allows the family as much time and space as needed.

- Do not be in a hurry, but rather offer care for each person.

- Practice as a care team the most appropriate words and phrases to say. The best response can just be, "I'm just so, so sorry for your loss."

- Practice as a care team how to address questions about cremation or regular burial.

- Be sure to let them know when or who will be calling from the church to help them with arrangements.

In the Days before the Service and the Day of the Service

As a team, be sure to spend time going over the protocol of what is expected of the care team in the days before the service as well as the day of the funeral. A few items you might consider:

- Have a plan for calling on the family, providing food if necessary.

- Decide how the CCMs can help with preparation for the service such as room setup.

- CCMs may be needed to offer care during a visitation or reception after the service.

- The day of the service, the CCMs are essential in their role to offer comfort and care throughout the day.

- In a time of social distancing, CCMs should feel comfortable and safe with whatever roles they might have.

- CCMs may be asked to read scripture or offer a few words during the service if they made multiple visits throughout the journey.

- Be alert for anyone who might be attending who may appear distressed or in need of comfort.

Follow-Up Care

Aftercare is so important following a death. Create a clear plan for follow-up, and take time as a team to evaluate how you can best offer care. A few ideas to consider:

- Make phone calls on a specific timetable.

- Send notes and cards on birthdays, anniversaries, holidays, and other special events when the family will especially be missing their loved one.

- Create a plan to send grief booklets (perhaps quarterly) that will include a personal note.

- CCMs can offer incredible leadership for any needed grief groups. Utilize vetted grief curriculum with healing theology that helps the grieving. Recommended titles include *Why* by Adam Hamilton, *Beyond the Broken Heart* by Julie Yarbrough, and *When the One You Love Is Gone* by Rebekah Miles.

God has given us a great opportunity to share the gospel message of hope during the dying process and at the time of death. Embrace your anointing to do this holy ministry, and it will bless you deeply!

And the one who was seated on the throne said, "See, I am making all things new." Also he said, "Write this, for these words are trustworthy and true."

—Revelation 21:5 NRSV

Notes, Reflections, and Ideas

Caring for People in Crisis and Trauma

The Advocate, the Holy Spirit, whom the Father will send in my name, will teach you everything, and remind you of all that I have said to you. Peace I leave with you; my peace I give to you. I do not give to you as the world gives. Do not let your hearts be troubled, and do not let them be afraid.

—John 14:25-27 NRSV

Definitions of Crisis and Trauma

Crisis is an acute situation; an emergency or circumstance of urgent need.

Trauma is the long-term effect of the crisis event.

THE FRAMEWORK FOR CARE
1. Talking points or information
2. Scriptures
3. Resources
4. Prayers or Words of Encouragement

Critical Care Situations

Anger

Talking Points/Facts

Anger is a trailhead that points to some hurt in a person's life. To find healing for that anger, direct the person to reflect on the following:

Why does this of all things make you so angry?

Follow that question until you find the wound that you tend to lock up.

Ask Jesus in prayer to heal that pain, which is using anger to feed it.

Schedule an appointment with either a pastor or a therapist to talk about the anger.

The goal is not to erase the hurt but to recognize it and find better ways of healing other than becoming angry.

Counting to ten, walking away, or giving yourself space can be helpful when enraged.

Scriptures

> Mark 1:40-41

> Hebrews 12:14-15

> Ephesians 4:29

> James 1:19

Prayer

> *Savior Jesus, my anger has not provided the healing, respect, and intimacy that I want. Forgive me for the ways that I have hurt others. I place the hurt that is causing my anger in your hands. Heal me, Lord Jesus. I need you. Amen.*

Suggested Reading and Resources

> *The Angry Book* by Theodore Rubin

> *Anger* by Gary Chapman

> *The Art of Forgiveness* by Lewis Smeeds

> *Forgiveness* by Lewis Smeeds

> *You're the One You've Been Waiting For* by Richard Schwartz

> *Angry God* by Michelle Novotini

> *The Dance of Anger* by Harriet Goldhor Lerner

Anger Management Classes

Provide the person a list of anger management classes, support groups, or other resources for learning and support.

Anxiety

Talking Points and Information

To find healing for anxiety, direct the person to reflect on the following:

Listen to the anxiety. What wisdom and instruction is it telling you?

- o   Some degree of anxiety can be good.

- o   Fear differs from anxiety.

- o   Legitimate fears have an object.

- o   Obsessive worry can cause unhealthy anxiety.

In the Bible, the Greek word for *anxiety* comes from two root words that mean "divide" and "mind."

Believe you are a child of God and that you are loved.

What is the root cause of your anxiety?

Can you name triggers, the things that cause you to be anxious?

Why would you stay stuck in anxiety patterns?

What is to be gained by being anxious? What is to be gained by giving up anxiety?

What would you do for God if you had no anxiety?

Name one thing that is overwhelming. Why is it so important?

Scriptures

Ephesians 3:20

Philippians 4:4-6

Hebrews 12:14-15

1 Peter 5:7-11

1 John 4:16-21

Genesis 1:31

Proverbs 3:5-6

Isaiah 43:1-5

Matthew 6:25-34

Romans 8:26-28

Prayer

Breath Prayer

Repeat one phase, such as "Be near me, Lord Jesus."

Take two or three deep breaths.

Repeat for two minutes.

ABC Prayer

Acknowledge

Breathe

Choose

Serenity Prayer

> God grant me the serenity
> to accept the things I cannot change;
> courage to change the things I can;
> and wisdom to know the difference.
>
> Living one day at a time;
> enjoying one moment at a time;
> accepting hardships as the pathway to peace;
> taking, as He did, this sinful world
> as it is, not as I would have it;
> trusting that He will make all things right
> if I surrender to His Will;
> that I may be reasonably happy in this life
> and supremely happy with Him
> forever in the next.
> Amen.
> —Reinhold Niebuhr

Suggested Reading and Resources

You Are the One You've Been Waiting For by Richard Schwartz

Anxiety Attacked: Apply Scriptures to the Cares of the Soul by John Macarthur Jr.

Embracing the Fear: Learning to Manage Anxiety and Panic Attacks by Judith Bemis

Fearless Relationships: Simple Rules for Lifelong Contentment by Karen Casey

The Breath of Life: A Simple Way to Pray by Ron DelBene

Paths to Prayer: Finding Your Own Way to the Presence of God by Patricia D. Brown

Coronavirus Anxiety Workbook by The Wellness Society

Live Well classes through Cor.org

Centers for Anxiety Treatment

Association for Adult Development and Aging (www.aadaweb.org)

Local church for pastoral counseling

Local community counseling specialist

Cancer and/or Chronic Illness

Talking Points/Facts

Love the physical part of you that carries the cancer or other chronic illness. Take care of it!

Focus on treatment opportunities.

Find joy within adversity when possible.

Ask supporters to be with you where you are—whether in pain or in joy as cheerleaders.

Scriptures

Psalm 121

Psalm 63:8

Isaiah 43:1-7

Lamentations 3:32

2 Corinthians 4:8

Philippians 4:13

Hebrews 12:2

James 5:13-15

1 Peter 5:7

Prayer

Lord, you said that when we walk through the water, you will be with us; we are precious in your sight and you love me. In this time of health trial and adversity, I need to be aware of your presence more than ever. Lord, some days I feel hard-pressed on every side, but with you near I do not feel crushed. I am struck down at times, but not destroyed. When this disease makes me feel as if I don't have any control, Lord, give me strength and courage, hold me in the palm of your hand, and give me peace. Amen.

Suggested Reading and Resources

Jesus Calling by Sarah Young

Jesus Lives by Sarah Young

The Will of God by Leslie Weatherhead

What about Divine Healing? by Susan Sonnenday Vogel

Cancer support groups

Ongoing pastoral care and counseling opportunities from the church

The American Cancer Society

Caring Conversations (www.practicalbioethics.org)

Depression

Talking Points/Facts

Listen to the message of depression. What is it trying to tell you?

Break the cycle of negative rumination that is part of depression.

What is good about you?

Who is in your support system?

Use helpful tools to combat depression:

- Exercise
- Omega-3 fatty acids
- Sunshine
- Social activity
- Sufficient rest
- A healthy diet

Scriptures

Job 19:7-10

Psalm 13:1-3

Psalm 34:18

Psalm 56

Proverbs 2:3-5

Isaiah 43:1-2, 5, 18-19

Luke 1:13

Philippians 4:13-14

Jeremiah 29:11

Prayer

Healing God, I celebrate your power to bring light to the darkness and healing and comfort to the brokenhearted. Your ways are mysterious, wonderful, and too vast for me to comprehend. As the Great Physician, be with me through moments of despair and hopelessness. Grant me hope and assurance that my life will be surrounded by your love and comfort. You are the God of hope. Give me the tools that will help me through this difficult journey. In Christ's name. Amen.

Suggested Reading and Resources

"When the World Seems Overwhelming: Dealing with Depression" (sermon) by Karen Lampe, May 22, 2005 UMC Church of the Resurrection, Sermon Archives

The Depression Cure by Dr. Steven Ilardi

Reaching for the Invisible God by Philip Yancey

The Freedom from Depression Workbook by Les Carter and Frank Minirth

Finding Hope Again by Neal Anderson and Hal Baumchen

Professional Counselor

Mental health questions at www.Godtest.com

Live Well Curriculum from COR.org

The Burns Depression Checklist (www.suicideforum.com/bdc /index.html)

Grief

Scriptures

Psalm 2

Isaiah 43:1-3

John 14:1-7

Romans 8

1 Corinthians 15

Revelation 21

Talking Points/Facts

Grief includes a sadness that is unique to and a natural response to loss. You can plan ways to grieve.

You can talk aloud with a trusted confidant (or write in a journal) about the feelings you're experiencing. In naming and being honest about all your feelings (which may be conflicting and seem irrational), you will recognize there is nothing wrong with your feelings.

How you choose to respond to your feelings is important (and this is critical work).

When you ask the "why" question (and you will), you will recognize that while there may be answers, those answers won't alleviate the nagging question, "Yes, but why my loved one?" You must recognize that this is normal.

When you become occupied with questions such as "Why me?" or "Why my loved one?" you might try asking aloud the opposite questions, which are, "Why not me? Why should I be exempt from these experiences that happen every day in this fallen world?"

When you ask God and yourself this question, you might be surprised (and helped) by the honest answers. Above all, remember that through the unconditional love of Jesus Christ, you are an Easter person; you are a person of the resurrection.

You will certainly grieve that you no longer have your loved one close to you, and you may have grief for what you perceive your loved one suffered prior to death; but, upon going through death, your loved one is in the shepherding arms and eternal care of God (Romans 8:35, 37-39).

Prayer

Lord, I need your grace and strength in order to be willing to move forward. I need the faith to believe you and I need the ability that you alone can give to release my loved one to your eternal care. Lord, help me be honest about my feelings and keep me from the tendency to choose bitterness and resentment. Grant me the grace to take one day at a time and to commit my feelings and memories to your eternal care. Help me celebrate and live with the good memories without remembering pain. Help me choose forgiveness so that one day I will see my loved one again. Amen.

Suggested Reading and Resources

Why? by Adam Hamilton

When the One You Love Is Gone by Rebekah L. Miles

Beyond the Broken Heart by Julie Yarbrough

A Long Shadowed Grief: Suicide and Its Aftermath by Harold Ivan Smith

When Grief Breaks Your Heart by James Moore

When a Child Dies, edited by Richard Hipps

And Then Mark Died by Susan Sonnenday Vogel

Grieving a Suicide by Albert Y. Hsu

What Do We Tell the Children? by Joseph Primo

Grief groups

Professional Counseling

Pastor

Divorce

Talking Points/Facts

> Your worth is not tied to your marital status. At your creation, God called you "very good."

> Divorce is a painful loss and will involve grieving.

> Dating immediately after a divorce can stifle the healing you need because you might try to find your healing in another person.

> You will need to eventually forgive, for your own sake. Forgiveness blesses you as you release the control your ex-spouse had over your feelings.

> Forgiving too soon can be hazardous to your healing. When you do forgive, you may decide to do it with your own ritual (for example, writing the word *forgiveness* on paper and burning it).

> Saying "I forgive you" to an ex-spouse often incites more anger and pain.

> If you are a parent, do not treat your kids, regardless of their ages, as your caregivers or best buddies.

> Make space for your kids (of all ages) to share their pain and grief even if their pain causes you guilt or hurt. They need you.

Teens may need particular attention during divorce: research shows that they are more likely to behave in overly sexualized ways or adopt an eating disorder or cut themselves.

Scriptures

Genesis 1:31

Philippians 3:12-15

Revelation 21:5

Luke 13:10-17

John 8:1-11

1 John 4:7-21

Hebrews 12:12-15

Romans 8:1

Prayer

God of infinite love and understanding, pour out your healing spirit upon me as I make a new beginning. Where there is hurt or bitterness, grant healing of memories and the ability to put behind me the things that are past. Where feelings of despair or worthlessness flood in, please nurture a spirit of hope. Give me confidence that, by your grace, tomorrow can be better than yesterday. Heal my children and help me minister to them. I pray for other family and friends in Jesus Christ my Savior. Amen.

Suggested Reading and Resources

> *Boundaries* by Henry Cloud and John Townsend, Zondervan Publishing House, 2017
>
> *Safe People* by Henry Cloud and John Townsend, Zondervan Publishing House
>
> *Radical Recovery: Transferring the Despair of Your Divorce into an Unexpected Good* by Suzy Brown
>
> Divorce recovery groups for men, women, and children
>
> Marriage and family therapists
>
> **Other categories of care** are included in the Care Cards available through The United Methodist Church of the Resurrection bookstore, The Well

Notes, Reflections, and Ideas

Mental Health Ministry

The LORD is near to the brokenhearted, and saves the crushed in spirit.

—Psalm 34:18 NRSV

As we do our part to help struggling people with their mental health, the faith community can be key to eliminating the stigmas and misunderstanding wrapped around mental health. Breaking the stigma can best be done through classes, sermons, and one-on-one care to help reduce the negative shame and denial.

List any stigmas you think hold people back from obtaining mental health care.

Key Ideas about Mental Health

- In almost all cases, mental health is a function of a chemical imbalance, plus a genetic predisposition, combined with environmental factors.

- MRI studies increasingly demonstrate that mental illness is best accounted for as differences in neurological functioning.

- 1 in 5 American adults experience a mental illness in a given year.

- Major mental illness reduces life expectancy by up to thirty years.

- 60 percent of people with mental illness do not receive treatment, usually because of stigmas.

What are the statistics for depression, anxiety, and suicide in your local area?

Key Symptoms of Depression

- Depressed mood

- Loss of interest or pleasure in all (or nearly all) activities

- A large increase or decrease in appetite/weight

- Insomnia or hypersomnia

- Slowing of physical movements or severe agitation

- Intense fatigue

- Excessive feelings of guilt or worthlessness

- Difficulty concentrating or making decisions

- Frequent thoughts of death or suicidality

    (Ilardi, Stephen, *The Depression Cure*, 2009)

Key Symptoms of Anxiety

- Excessive worrying

- Panic, fear, and restlessness

- Sleep problems

- Not being able to stay calm or still.

- Cold, sweaty, numb, or tingling hands or feet.

- Shortness of breath

- Heart palpitations

- Dry mouth

- Nausea

Prayer

Prayer and meditation can be very helpful tools as we offer nonjudgmental compassion and connection to God. Also just the gift of being present and listening can offer assurance that the person is worthy and valued. As you offer care, model good boundaries and life skill habits. Here is a sample prayer:

Living God, open my heart that I may connect to your Spirit. Lord, I acknowledge that I am feeling fearful, overwhelmed, anxious, and depressed. Help me to remember that I am your precious child and that you want me to live a full life. God of healing grace, help me to breathe deeply as I breathe in your peace and exhale any pain or anxiety that I may be experiencing. God, help me to visualize your light and love reaching out to me that I may find new peace, comfort, and assurance that you are with me. Help me to choose life, that I may fight for my life and find the right fellowship of others who will help me during this challenging time. All this I pray in Christ's name. Amen.

Care for People Having Suicidal Thoughts

Talking Points and Information

Contemplating suicide can be the result of untreated depression, anxiety, or untreated pain and suffering. Some of the main drivers of suicide include PTSD, thwarted love, fractured control, assaulted self-image, and the rupture of a key relationship.

If you are suicidal seek help immediately.

Create a plan with a trusted pastor or counselor including whom to call if you are suffering.

Remember you are a precious child of God.

Helpful Scriptures

Deuteronomy 30:19-20

Deuteronomy 31:8

Psalm 139:14

Romans 8:35

Psalms 23; 27; 28; 31; 40

John 10:10

Philippians 4:4-9, 13

Ephesians 6:10-20

Suggested Reading and Resources

Let Your Life Speak by Parker Palmer

Suicide Hotline: 1-800-SUICIDE

Call 911

www.suicidepreventionlifeline.com

www.musicforthesoul.org

Live Well curriculum: http://www.cor.org/ministries/care-and -support/live-well/

Depression interview with Dr. Stephen Ilardi: http://www.cor.org /ministries/care-and-support/live-well/depression-interview/

Key Care for Survivors of Suicide

Talking Points/Information

God is the great parent and did not cause this death.

It is no one's fault.

Chemical imbalance can cause irrational thinking.

"Why would he/she do this to us?" is a normal question.

"Took his life" or "completed suicide" is theologically a better choice of wording than "committed suicide," which links it to a sinful act.

The United Methodist Church believes that nothing, including suicide, can separate us from the love of God (Romans 8:35-38).

Talk out loud with a trusted pastor, counselor, or caregiver about the emotions you are experiencing.

Remember above all else that we are Easter people and that the unconditional love of God will see us through this event.

Suicide care requires a team effort of pastors, counselors, and a helpful grief group.

Scriptures

Psalm 34:18

John 3:16

John 10:28

Romans 8:35-38

Suggested Readings

Why? by Adam Hamilton

A Long Shadowed Grief: Suicide and Its Aftermath by Harold Ivan Smith

Take the Dimness of My Soul Away: Healing after a Loved One's Suicide by William Ritter

When Bad Things Happen to Good People by Harold S. Kushner

The Will of God by Leslie D. Weatherhead

Resources

Local grief ministry or contact the grief ministry at The United Methodist Church of the Resurrection

Local grief counselors and groups

Continued connection to pastor or theologically trained caregiver

Notes, Reflections, and Ideas

Addiction Care

Save me, O God, for the waters have come up to my neck.
I sink in deep mire,
where there is no foothold;
I have come into deep waters,
and the flood sweeps over me.
I am weary with my crying;
my throat is parched.
My eyes grow dim
with waiting for my God.

With your faithful help rescue me from sinking in the mire.

—Psalm 69:1-3, 13b-14 NRSV

What are your local resources for recovery?

How can you create a recovery ministry in your church?

Talking Points and Information

There is a need for the person to have the will to recover. The addict's ownership of the problem and intention to begin to recover has to come first.

Acknowledge the dependence on alcohol, drugs, pornography, and so forth.

There are people who can walk alongside you on this journey. They may be in recovery from their own journeys.

You can live a new life in Christ.

Love yourself: you are a child of God. Shaming yourself does not help.

Set aside a disciplined time and place to work on your addiction.

Scriptures

Romans 7:15-20

Romans 8:28

Romans 12:1

Lamentations 3:40

James 4:10

1 John 1:9

1 John 5:14-15

Matthew 11:28-30

Philippians 3:12-16

Suggested Readings

Nurturing the Light Inside: Overcoming Addiction and Codependency on the Path to Self-Love by Sherry Danner

Intervention: How to Help Someone Who Doesn't Want Help by Vernon Johnson

Addict in the Family: Stories of Loss, Hope, and Recovery by Beverly Conyers

Codependent No More: How to Stop Controlling Others and Start Caring for Yourself by Melody Beattie

Life Healing Choices: Freedom from Your Hurts, Hang-Ups, and Habits by John Baker

The Alcoholics Anonymous Big Book 4th ed, by AA Services

Rational Recovery: The New Cure for Substance Addiction by Jack Trimpey

Resources

Alcoholic Anonymous: www.aa.org

Narcotics Anonymous: www.na.org

Al Anon: www.al-anon.alateen.org

Recovery Ministry at COR.org

Notes, Reflections, and Ideas

Critical Communal Trauma

All who believed were together and had all things in common; they would sell their possessions and goods and distribute the proceeds to all, as any had need.

—Acts 2:44 NRSV

Examples of Communal Trauma

- Pandemic
- Financial crisis
- Food Insecurity
- Weather disasters (hurricane, wildfire, tornadoes)
- Hate crimes and discrimination
- Mass shootings

Immediate Responses

Go to the scene if you can safely be present.

Work as a team.

Listen.

Attend to physical needs.

Offer scripture and prayer when appropriate.

Make a plan for next steps.

Collaborate with other local care institutions and agencies as appropriate.

Responses through the Trauma

Abide by local, state, and national guidelines.

Call on denominational leaders for resources, financial assistance, and first responders.

Communicate, communicate, communicate with your congregation and local leaders.

Check in and follow up with those most affected.

Create trauma follow-up programs that include mental health professionals.

Restore and continue weekly worship with helpful theology.

Create care classes such as prayer and grief groups.

Attend to financial assistance with community leaders.

Creatively utilize volunteers' skills for new needs such as face masks, sandbags (for flooding), food banks, and construction crews.

Consider Long-Term Responses and Changes

How you offer worship and classes

Long-term follow-up plan as a team

Spiritual and emotional care

Long-term plan for financial care

Collaborative planning with community leaders about housing assistance

Questions for Reflection

- What has your church learned going through communal trauma?

- Are you better prepared to address another challenge?

- How can your denomination help?

- What ways can you work collaboratively with others in your community?

Notes, Reflections, and Ideas

Made in the USA
Monee, IL
18 May 2022